FROM MUCK
to
Magnificence

How Cleaning Horse Stalls
Can Lead to an Astonishing Life

MINDY TATZ CHERNOFF

Preface

$\mathcal{W}$riting a book, allowing what is inside you to emerge and turn into a printed page, is an incredibly daunting task. Researchers have said we are "wired for connection." Recognizing this, I see my life as a compilation of every person I have met, as well as those who, simply by a glance or a smile, may have impacted my heart. And I feel tremendous gratitude for *all* the connections and "chance" encounters in my life thus far.

Which brings me to the four-legged connections — *horses*. My life has been a love fest of saying "Yes!" to them since I was eight years old. (Earlier, really, as you shall soon see, but eight was when I received my first pony.) Buck did not stay long, but Rocky! Oh, he was with me for years. He was one of my greatest teachers. I remember when we moved him to a new boarding stable. I was so excited; I hopped on him and immediately hit the trails. I was nine and I fell off of him *three times* that day! Of course, each and every time, I hopped back on! Fast forward to today...I have had parents remove their children from riding classes because they had fallen off the horse. They weren't injured; they just took a tumble. It speaks volumes of how we raise our children, what levels of discomfort we allow, or do not allow, in their lives—in *our* lives.

From Buck to Rocky to Buck Jones to Ki to Snickers, Ginger, Coffee, and Viton. In between were scores of horses bought and sold. Some stayed and were bought by students...they were the cream of the crop! Some of them I struggled with, and my most impactful lessons were learned from them. Every one of these horses was beautiful in its own way, created by a marvelous, diverse Creator. These four-legged Master Teachers have informed and shaped the woman I am today. I am forever grateful. I hope the words in this book about these wonderful creatures and the lessons I learned from them will inform and inspire you, too.

Perhaps after you have read *From Muck to Magnificence*, you will experience firsthand how these principles can transform your life. This book is based on the healing methods used at The Resonant Horse, my private horse farm outside of Philadelphia, Pennsylvania. There, skilled facilitators partner with horses to offer clarity, transformation, and freedom to clients from diverse backgrounds and life experiences. The horses are the Master Teachers; we are granted the privilege to partner with them as they aid us in transforming and becoming the best and most free versions of ourselves that we can be!

The Resonant Horse offers workshops, retreats, and one-on-one sessions at the farm. In addition, I am available for speaking engagements and phone-coaching sessions. Whether one is a skilled equestrian or has never been around a horse, The Resonant Horse can speak to many demographics. Equine-facilitated learning can aid us to:

- Become more authentic and grounded
- Live with an open heart
- Acquire tools to deal better with our discomfort
- Access our hidden leadership skills
- Gain healthy coping skills as we connect with the horse's world
- Learn appropriate boundaries and how to say no
- Understand the difference between attachment and nonattachment personality relationship styles
- Gain greater emotional intelligence, which is great training for corporate and executive leadership roles
- Learn how to accept and let go
- And that is just the beginning!

Because partnering with horses is often felt deeply within the heart, at times it is challenging to put it into words. But words, as limited as they are, are the way we humans express what is occurring most deeply within us. I can, however, tell you a story that, by analogy, describes rather well how horses impact our lives.

I was driving into the city one day and proceeded to park at a spot that had a kiosk. You exit your car, head over to a kiosk, pay the fee, and receive a ticket for the amount of time you intend to be parked. You place the ticket on the front dash of your car. My appointment ran short, and I had one and a half hours remaining on my ticket.

"What to do with it?" I wondered. As I backed

out, I saw a gentleman pulling into a spot next to me.

I rolled down my window and asked him, "Are you going to be here for about one and one half hours?"

He responded very curtly and suspiciously, with a perturbed air about him, "Yes, why?"

"Here," I said, and I reached out my hand and handed him my ticket. "This is for you. It is good for one and one half hours."

In that instant, in a moment, that gentleman's heart went from completely closed to wide open.

He broke into a *huge* smile and said, "Thank you so much!"

As I drove away, so pleased I could bless another, the feeling of connection and touching another's life lingered with me. It was not a foreign emotion; it was one that I often felt. And, as I pondered, I realized, *this is what horses do for us!* They take closed hearts, and they *open* them. All the time. Every day. All we need to do is show up. And be curious. As one of my students said: "Understanding horses helps me to understand people!"

This is what we do at The Resonant Horse!

For more information on The Resonant Horse, visit Theresonanthorse.com.

You can also view the TEDX Talk that I discuss in the book at: https://youtube/QBZkFqulqog

Acknowledgments

$\mathcal{I}$ am incredibly grateful to my parents who raised me and to my sister with whom I grew up. We both had the love of horses in our veins early on. I went the quarter horse/Appaloosa route; she went the Arabian route. Horses were clearly in our genes, as you shall surely see.

I am even more thankful for my children. I am filled with gratitude and awe as I see the amazing adults you have become and are still becoming. Sharon, Aron, Elisha, all of you are a gift to whomever you come into contact with. My love for you is deep and fierce. Thank you to Joel, their father, for partnering in raising them. Thank you to their spouses for loving them so deeply.

My eyes fill with tears of gratitude as I ponder the journey so many have shared with me. I also know that by listing friends and family some will unintentionally be left out. Please accept my apologies. We are a compilation of all we have met, and through the years, some of my most pivotal relationships have been with these people who will forever be in my heart:

Carol M.; Susan H.; Sally W.; Elisa Joy T.; Winnie and Mark F. and their children, Lori B., Rob, and Andi S.; Mike and Tara S.; Paul and Luanne W.; Faith and Peter Y.; Liz P.; DJS; Bobby Jo V.; Sita N.; Shari J.; Dr. Jeff; Stan and Ellen B.; Annie M.; Connie P.; Dr. Dan.; Dave and Miho; Margie M.; Natasha C.; Ajit M.G.; Sarah B.; Jac and Janna C.; Rose A.; Ariel G.;

Dr. Joel E.; Dr. John B.; Dr. Steve and Chris S.; Kris D.; Melinda G; Pete and Linda C.; Keri R.; Veronica and Abe; Andrew and Kathy. L.; Terri and Bob G.; Shoshanna L.; Dr. Jo; Dr. Peter B.; Drew S.; Caroline W.; Paul G. and the Hatton, Rosenberg and Rosenthal families.

You have all believed in me when I could not believe in myself. You have helped to open a heart that was suffering and closed. My great thanks go to *all* of you.

To Brent and Kris Graef and to Linda Kohanov: Your kindness, wisdom, and adoration for horses encourage me to be like you. Thank you for your friendship.

To *all* my students: You know who you are! Julie, Bev, Sally, Tracy, Ariel, Karly, Jackie, the list goes on and on! Your childhood was shaped and formed by Timonium horse auctions, horse shows, and camp field trips to Amish horse auctions and saddle shops! What wonderful times we had!

To my clients: You have opened your hearts to me and allowed the horses to transfigure and transform your suffering. A thank you seems insufficient. I become mute, deeply silent and still, when confronted with your courage. My heart overflows with gratitude. Gratitude makes one feel more open, more generous, and more alive. Thank you for eliciting this wonderful emotion within me.

I am compelled to offer another set of thanks: To those clients who have come with heavy hearts, who have experienced the healing power of the horses, but who have for some reason chosen to say "no," I also owe my utmost respect to you. I will honor your need to walk away. You leave a lingering thought:

"What could the horses and I have done to change your 'no' into a 'yes'?" I hope one day we will see you again. That is my quest; that we all can and will say "Yes!" to the horses...to ourselves.

Introduction

What Inspired Me to Partner with Horses

You may be wondering what inspired me to begin partnering with horses as a way to help people gain more clarity, freedom, and power. I found myself wondering the same thing when I was about to begin writing this book. To seek the answer, I turned to the pages of my past.

I decided to revisit some of my old journals. I gave myself a complete afternoon and evening to write. Instead, I procrastinated. I watched TV. I watered my plants. I picked snow peas from my garden. I swam. I made dinner. I played with the dogs. I wrote on Facebook how I was procrastinating. I read all the comments on Facebook on my procrastination.

Finally, I succumbed and surrendered to the moment. I said "yes" to the process. In so doing, as I scrolled through the pages of my past, I found threads of my future. "The Resonant Horse," unnamed as of yet, was being birthed.

I discovered the moment of inspiration in a letter from an old friend, Deb, after a day at my farm. She had connected beautifully with the horses that day. She writes: "My time at the farm was wonderful...I was so blessed to have that day...I know you believe in healing with these animals, as I do. You are the reason I get to have these days. I thank God everyday for you and your generous spirit."

From very early on, I saw that the horses were transforming lives, one barn visit at a time. Some of my journal entries also spoke of challenges and pain: "One way to enlarge the soul is through grief and loss. When we are hurting, we are anxious. When we are anxious, we tend to stay away from situations. Don't isolate yourself; become part of a herd."

Years ago, two tenets of The Resonant Horse were visible:

1. Be present to your suffering. If you can stay open and curious, which is how horses live, you can expand your attitude and live with being more present to your suffering and to your joys. Especially to your suffering. Connecting with others and yourself is key.

2. Saying "yes." Saying "yes" is easy when all is going our way. However, we all have triggers that make it challenging to move forward by avoiding harsh and critical self-judgment.

To fully embrace every moment, even in discomfort, takes courage and trust.

Eventually, I knew I was going to sit down and write, which I did. And along the way, plants got watered, dogs were played with, and I received the bounty from the garden. All was exactly as it was meant to be. I was conscious of feeling gratitude in every moment.

Stop right now. Look up from the pages you are reading. Look at your surroundings. You have sight. You have breath. You have (I hope) a relatively healthy body. You are loved. In this moment, life is a gift. And life is good. Setting your intention in this moment toward gratitude is a wonderful thing. In this exact moment, you have everything you need.

If you feel that, in this moment, that life is less than perfect, you can still say "yes" and thanks. Even if you do not feel this way—particularly if you do not feel this way—express it anyway.

You see, many people live in an either/or mindset. It is not only constricting, it creates distance and separation. For example:

- You are either a friend or a foe.
- You are either a Democrat or a Republican or an Independent or a Libertarian.
- You are of my religion or you are not.
- The alternative is the both/and mind-set:
- You are different from me and I can accept diversity.
- I may be suffering and I can see the invitation toward growth that my suffering provides and am thankful.

The both/and mind-set is not particularly new. Comedians doing improv have been assimilating it into their scripts for years! A short time ago, I took two improv classes. I was astounded to see these principles used as an integral part of improv comedy. There are even books written on how these principles can influence leaders and executives!

Improv is all about saying "yes" to whatever your comedy partner is saying and doing. It does not stop there. With improv, you say "yes/and!" no matter what your partners or fellow comedians are saying; that is how you respond. You enlarge upon whatever is unfolding in the moment, in the skit. It is a mindset of not only saying "yes" to the opportunity, but adding your own enthusiasm and comedic input to the skit as it unfolds in the present moment.

So you see the correlation? We, too can approach the skits of our lives with open, curious hearts. Responding with being present and with depth to whatever unfolds during our days is how horses live, day after day. We already know they respond and react accordingly to whatever stimuli they meet up with in the moment.

We too can do the same.

> If we are in pain due to a relationship, if we are feeling deeply, it speaks of our love toward another. It is a wonderful thing. It speaks of connection. And, connection is what we are invited to do, over and over again. Horses get it. They live in herds that are imperative to their survival. It is all about connecting.

Remember Deb, my friend I spoke of at the beginning of this introduction? Recently, she brought a colleague, Jess, out to the farm. This particular day was filled with energy, motion, and people. I had a new employee learning the ropes. We had an extra dog running around and playing. A new student had arrived. It was busy!

In the midst of it all, Deb took Jess to the round pen with one of the horses. A round pen is a fenced-in circle, approximately 60 feet in diameter, where horses and humans can interact in a secure environment. It is where much of the partnering with horses occurs, through exercises and experiences.

As Jess and Duke were in the round pen, I stopped over by the fence. I was distracted by all that was going on in that moment, but I paused and took notice. In that instant, Duke was modeling true connection as he followed Jess around with no halter, no lead rope, just by the love in Jess's heart. He followed her around like a puppy dog. It was a beautiful thing to watch.

I said to Jess: "I don't know what you are going through in your life right now. I don't know who has said 'no' to you in your life, but in this instant, you have 1,250 pounds saying 'yes' to you. In this moment, the only place Duke wants to be is with you."

Occasionally, I may say something to someone and not have a clue how it affected them. Jim Carrey said that "the most effective form of currency is the impact your life has upon another." Such was my comment to Jess. Later that day, she contacted me and mentioned her experience. Very eloquently, she spoke of her session with Duke:

"Hi ya, beautiful! I just wanted to extend my sincerest gratitude for you allowing me to spend the day on your incredible farm yesterday. The experience had a profound impact on me and completely changed my life perspective. Duke has such a stunning and powerful presence and I am genuinely grateful to have spent some time with him. Horses are truly magical creatures and I firmly believe that they are remarkably therapeutic and have the power to heal parts of your soul that you may not even realize are broken.

I have been struggling a lot lately with self-esteem and just feeling as small and insignificant as humanly possible for reasons that stem from past experiences that unfortunately still haunt my life. Duke following me and allowing me to connect with him was one of the most humbling moments I have ever experienced. I could not stop smiling and just feeling so thankful to be alive...a feeling that has been missing for the past few months.

Just being in his presence allowed me to forget the ugly in this world and focus all of my energy on the beauty right in front of me. You said something to me in that moment that made my heart lay flat on the floor. You said: 'When you feel like everyone else is saying no, here is 1,250 lb. saying yes. You are the only one in the world at this moment that he wanted to be around.'

That hit me like a ton of bricks and it took every single part of me not to break down and cry. To feel special and appreciated by such a gorgeous being made me feel like, for the first time in my life, I was enough. Not skinnier, not prettier. Not wealthier. Just as I am."

Jess connecting with Duke gave her the gift of trust—trusting the horse, trusting herself. She can now continue to blossom into the best version of herself. The person who feels deeply connects wholeheartedly and shares that love with others.

What a beautiful example of how The Resonant Horse heals, transforms, and empowers. Jess is one of scores of others who have said "Yes!" to the power of these magnificent animals who woo us to become the truest and most loving versions of ourselves. It would be impossible to say "No" to such an invitation! An astonishing life awaits *you!*

Chapter 1

My Early Involvement–and Gift!–of Being with Horses

$\mathcal{I}$ was five years old with cat-eye glasses for my big brown eyes and wearing spandex pants. I was riding in my first horse show. It was an indoor arena at Holdorff Riding Academy, near my home in the northwest suburbs of Chicago. Four riders were in the class. I placed second. Later, I was told that I did not win because the announcer had asked us to make a circle to the right. Not knowing my left from my right, I turned the wrong way! I kept that second-place ribbon for many, many years.

Even though I was riding at the tender age of five, my involvement with horses and the "fertilizer" they leave began earlier, much earlier.

My mom and her sister were privileged back in the late '40s to have a car to drive to high school. One day, they drove up to the high school campus and parked near the school alongside some rather fancy homes. As they were leaving the car, a woman came out and said, "You can't park here. We do not let kikes park here." ("Kike" was a derogatory term for a Jewish person back in the day.)

At dinner that evening, Mom and her sister asked their father, "Daddy, what is a 'kike'?"

He explained that it was an unkind term used to describe Jews. As my mom, just a teenager at the time, described the incident, her father (my eventual grandfather) asked her to please get him the address of the woman who had spoken it to them.

The following day, Grampie had a truckload

of horse manure dumped on her front lawn. The woman never called them "kikes" again. You see, my grandfather Hy had connections. From the '40s through the '70s, he was part of the Jewish mob in Chicago. Finding a stable in need of dumping its manure was not difficult for him. Like I said, I go back, way back, with manure.

Because my life with horses began so young, the continual care they required was a given. My mom always said I kept my barn cleaner than my room. And she was right. She may still be right when I think about it! I grew up with a strong work ethic as I tended to and took care of my pony and the horse I eventually had. No way to know how many stalls I have "mucked" (cleaned) out, but it must be somewhere in the thousands.

While I was not aware of it at the time, mucking those stalls was planting seeds—seeds of connection. I was training my brain; by tending to and caring for horses, I was making neural connections.

> Having an integrative relationship with an animal where your involvement is experienced on several levels stimulates the integration of neural connections in the brain.

In addition, secure, healthy attachments also promote integration of neural connections in the brain. So, at an early age, I was changing my brain. I was in a safe environment, connecting with something much larger than me that needed daily care. I was learning about myself. I was learning about these exquisite animals. What a gift this was, being with horses!

Thought Questions

At the end of every chapter, there are questions and exercises that guide you into deeper personal exploration. I use similar questions like them at my workshops and retreats. Answer them slowly, thoughtfully. Allow the questions to linger with you. Let The Resonant Horse transform you, right where you are now!

Introduction Thought Questions

1. Can you recall a "chance encounter" in your life? How did it affect you? What decision and/or clarity did it offer you?

2. If you are a parent, can you recall an experience with your child that resulted in feelings of discomfort?

3. How did you respond/react? Was the situation resolved? If not, why not? What is the deeper invitation here? If the situation was resolved, how did it affect future moments of discomfort?

4. Make a list of ten people in your life who adore you just the way you are. Repeat each name out loud. As you do, offer a prayer of gratitude and thanks to each person for being a support in your life.

5. It has been said that the most powerful moments in our lives cannot be seen or touched but are felt in the heart. List an experience you have had that was so impactful it brought you to stillness and silence. Please share.

6. Have you ever had an opportunity to say "Yes" to a growth experience and you instead said "No"? How did that turn out for you? What could it have looked like if you had said "Yes" instead? Can you look at both options with a lens of gentleness and kindness toward yourself? If not, why not?

Chapter 1 Thought Questions

1. List five strong principles you were raised with.

2. Which of those principles do you still hold today? Which ones do you not believe or follow?

3. Why have some remained with you? Why have some not?

4. If you are a parent, which principles do you feel should be passed on to your children?

Chapter 2

Mucking a Stall, 101

*W*orking with horses involves much more than just riding them. There are many mundane chores to do when one says "yes" to horses. A daily routine of care is paramount and necessary to maintain the animal's well-being and health. If done incorrectly, it can negatively impact the animal. Regardless of whether the horse is stalled for long periods of time or only occasionally, a stall needs daily tending to. I used to clean my stalls *twice* a day. Some stables clean them more often than that, others less. It is imperative that one removes the manure and urine from the stall. You then "bed" with various kinds of materials or bedding for the comfort and well-being of the horse.

When I was younger, I would allow my foolish impatience to take precedence—how fast could I clean the stalls? Now, I find myself slowing down, not being in a rush, lingering.

> When you have a chore, a routine, mundane one, there is only one way for it to *not* be mundane and routine: to do that routine task with great love and care.

I have the privilege to model this behavior, that of slowing down and doing a routine task with great care. Occasionally, I have students arrive from the inner city. There, life is rather different than at the farm. Because of that, they are much more reactionary; they are wired to be in the flight or fight mode all the time. Their stress levels are high; they do tasks very quickly and oftentimes just react and rush through them. So I explain to them that for today, we will do something that may seem counterintuitive to them. We are not going to rush through the task, whatever it may be. Perhaps it is cleaning the stall. Instead of scurrying through the task, we are going to slow down. Linger. We are going to see how *long* it can take to clean the stall. Doing so allows their busy brains to slow down and hopefully return to a state of more satiation instead of high stress.

I model for them the behavior, and then I allow them to experience it. Cleaning the stall then becomes a routine task, but one done with great care and love.

How can that happen? How does one go from rushing and moving fast to slowing down, stopping, and noticing? It is not that difficult, but it does take some intention and attention—attention to every movement as well as to thoughts racing in the mind. And the intention to change, to be willing to allow something else to replace the fast-paced, "monkey mind" and slow down and stop. That, my friends, is a way to be transformed. It is a way to a magnificent life. Come along...

First, Choose Your Bedding

Much of horse stall mucking, initially anyway, depends on the bedding you use in the stall. My favorite when I was little was corncob bedding. The cobs were in small pieces, and I loved the color, the size, the absorbency. It is very difficult to find today. Years ago, I used to head out to Lancaster County, PA, with a bunch of students to a corncob factory. There, we would climb atop an enormous, huge dump truck that held twenty-five tons and scoop or shovel the corncobs into huge, plastic bags. I am still amazed that the company would let me and the children do that! Fast forward to today; I am doubtful that in this day and age of lawsuits you could do this now.

Shavings were my next favorite type of bedding. I just loved the wonderful odor of fresh cedar shavings. For the stall muckers of today, pelleted bedding is the current rage. This bedding consists of small pellets that hold moisture and double or triple in size when wet. They are very absorbent and do not have any strong urine odor.

There are alternate types of bedding, like straw or shredded paper. Both, in my opinion, do not absorb as well as shavings or pellets. Sawdust is another type of bedding but is very dusty, so it's not a good choice for humans or horses with allergies.

How to Clean a Horse Stall

First, it is best to remove the horse from the stall. I know I may be stating the obvious, but to move around a horse with a pitchfork (or apple picker as they are fondly called today) is not safe. Once the 1,250-pound distraction is removed, take your apple picker and go in. In my early years, pitchforks were always metal with sharp tines. Present-day "apple pickers" are often plastic and have tines with blunt ends. It is nice that as time has gone on, styles have softened. For our purposes, the blunt ends are preferable.

Using the apple picker, pick up the manure and wet bedding. For solid manure (poop), lift the manure away from the remainder of the bedding and shake it—sift it a bit. This allows the good bedding to return to the stall, while the solid residue stays on the apple picker. Last, place the solid residue in a wheelbarrow or bucket, however you choose to dispose of it. Remove the muck and let go, placing it in the container of your choice. If you want to, add a small amount of lye or lime material that absorbs the urine odor in the stall.

Then, spread another bag or two of pellets on the floor of the clean stall. Eyeball it as to whether or not you need to add another bag of bedding. Also, different types of bedding require different thicknesses in the stall. With shavings and straw, you can have a nice, deep bed in the stall, so you can add more. However, avoid making a deep bed of wood pellets. When wet, the pellets absorb so much moisture that they become almost impossible to lift! Way too heavy! So, you bed "light."

There are many ways to dispose of manure. Certainly the way my grandfather did it would not be a very wise option! Some companies will take it for fertilizer and provide a large container to place the manure in, thus storing and allowing the manure to decompose and then spreading it as fertilizer, which is also an option for those people who have a lot of acreage. The wonderful thing about manure is how it can be repurposed. Nothing is wasted!

Now that you are all stall-cleaning experts...let's dive deeper into the magnificent muck!

Chapter 2 Thought Questions

1. What "chores" or repetitive actions do you have in your life? How do you view them?

2. What would it look like for you to linger and be present to each task, one after the other?

3. Can you view each task with great care and love? If so, what does that feel like?

Chapter 3

Pick and Choose

$\mathcal{T}$he first tool to take you from *Muck to Magnificence* is picking.

Picking connotes choosing. You have to have an element of discernment for when, what, and whom you pick and choose. However, something must happen even before you pick and choose.

You must know, deep in your gut, and believe you are

WORTHY
VALUABLE
and CHOSEN.

So, when I say we are chosen, I speak of having a deep knowing that we are loved and cherished by a Power much greater than ourselves.

Chosen by whom, you might ask? Well, from my perspective and outlook, I see such tremendous diversity in people, in nature, and in animals; the Universe just oozes with creation—magnificent creation. Taking that one step further: If the world is filled with creation, that speaks of a Creator. So, when I say we are chosen, I speak of having a deep knowing that we are loved and cherished by a Power much greater than ourselves. Simply put, there is a God, and we are not him or her. This is foundation-al, for it sets the tone for the way we live, move, and walk on this earth. It even impacts in nonverbal ways our presence when we meet another living creature.

It even affects how you "pick" your stall. As you muck the stall, you are "manure picking"; you are choosing what needs to be removed and what is good to leave behind. You are moving toward what is healthy and correct and life giving. You are moving away from what is not necessary—the debris of your life, so to speak. As you are mucking the stall, you pick what needs to be removed. This is a great intention for life as well. Horses are wonderful for aligning us with what is most life giving within us.

Horses are masters of nonverbal intention. Their heart rates will change in the presence of someone who is nervous or agitated. To a horse, nervousness or anxiety translates as a form of predatory power, and it makes them want to flee from it.

Altering heart rates works both ways, however. If our intention is one of love and an open heart, we can allow the horse's calm and large energy field to slow down *our* own heart rates. Many of my clients come to the farm in an agitated state; life is very stressful these days. By being in the presence of horses, they move into a more relaxed and peaceful state of being.

One friend who came to visit sat down on a chair in the barn and said, "I don't know what it is, but I just want to stay here! I feel so calm." Horses live in a satiated state (unless provoked by their surroundings) and ooze calmness and peace. That makes it easier for us to choose to be present in places that offer comfort and peace, too.

At times, it may be difficult to know what to choose. "Poop Patrol" is obvious, very cut-and-dry—

you remove the manure (or debris) and keep the good stuff, that is, the bedding. But for us humans, in our lives, choosing can be complicated: "What do I need to move toward?" "What do I need to move away from?"

Sometimes, tiny things get in the way. One tried-and-true method (and we are really talking about *discernment*, here) is to move towards love. Always move towards love. Remaining open and curious is also key. In addition, you will not be able to choose effectively, if you are manifesting judgment that is directed toward yourself or others. Judging is *so* pervasive in our society. On a personal level, many people are relentlessly harsh on themselves. I know, because I used to be one of them.

In addition, judging feeds the fuel of entitlement and separation, all the while exalting the ego of the one standing in judgment. Some people have an internal clock of such extreme self-judgment that it literally emerges encased in sarcastic humor. Using belittling humor, they exalt themselves while making others feel bad. If you are aware, you can feel it. You may laugh at their humor, but there is something deep inside of you, a knowing, that makes you cringe. A small part of you is sad inside because you feel bad for the person the joke or comment is directed toward. Such comments speak loudly about the person who issued the joke; he or she is looking through his or her own lens of excruciating self-judgment. People like this are suffering and most likely do not even know it. They need our compassion.

For such people, at the time they tell the joke or say the comment, it does one thing: It lifts themselves up while making the other feel "less than." Remember, it is all about *picking and choosing*. If you find yourself in the place of feeling "less than," return to the wondrous sensation of knowing you are chosen, loved, and valued just the way you are. *Especially* because of the way you are. If you are making yourself feel "less than," you must get out of your mind. It is a bad neighborhood!

Sometimes, it is the horses that gently and kindly show us what needs to be seen. Sarah (not her real name) is a lovely woman and mother who recently came out to the barn for her first session. As she was spending time with one of the horses, she became quiet. I asked her what she was feeling. She said she was sad and wondered if the horse was feeling and taking on her sadness.

I responded, "Well, he may be, but what about your good attributes? Is it possible that he is also taking on your *good* traits?"

As she reflected on this, she said: "This is something I apparently have been overlooking for a very long time. It is very hard for me to recognize and praise the good traits about myself. It is so easy for me to constantly nitpick myself and all the things I am doing wrong—or think I am doing wrong—and I never give myself any credit for the things that I do right or the positive traits I have. I guess it correlates to my lack of confidence in myself. It is something I have been working on for a long time, and I am just struggling to get there. I am so very thankful that my experience in the barn helped point that out."

This is a beautiful example of how the horses can inform our lives in a way that is nonjudgmental and kind. Of course, I could explain to Sarah how we are wired to think negatively; it is a leftover of our early wiring from our prehistoric ancestors. They *had* to be able to notice negative things because their lives depended on it. Today, we do not need to have the same focus, but our neurons are wired to emphasize the negative. The wonderful thing is we can change that! By *choosing* to focus on the good, we can alter our wiring to allow for more gratitude, acceptance, and joy in our lives.

Of course, in that instance, Sarah did not care about such things. She was only there with a horse in a moment where light was shed on her experience. She told me that as she continued her visit, "I carried the calm feeling with me throughout the rest of my day. I honestly felt like my heart was beating at a steady, gentle pace; it was an incredible feeling."

Yes, the horses are the Master Teachers. In just one moment, a young woman gained a profound awareness of how her life could be altered, how she could change the negative tapes that played in her mind.

When I find myself getting bogged down by the internal tapes playing negative scripts in my own mind, I work diligently to alter my brain connections. To rewire my brain, I have to make a shift. Sometimes, it is a huge shift—a move into a different room, taking a walk, lingering with a horse. Other times, the shift is small, possibly imperceptible to others. I become still, quiet. I recall that as a child of God, I am loved, adored, and cherished. I return to my body. I breathe; I stop, and I notice. Inevitably, I am brought to a place of gratitude and thankfulness. I say a prayer of thanks for the exact moment I am in, however the external circumstances may appear.

Gratitude and judgment cannot coexist. *So,* draw yourself toward the gratitude, which will return you toward choosing love.

You may have to remind yourself to do this daily, even many times a day with no lens of judgment. Simply do the next thing that needs tending to with great love. And be thankful. Always be thankful.

Sometimes, life may interrupt us, and lessons may present more of a challenge to embrace. A short time ago, I had a conversation with a dear friend. It involved her personal life and some choices she felt she needed to make for her well-being. The choice she was moving toward was one that I intuitively knew she was going to make. In fact, I had known for a while.

Sometimes, I feel that I get insight and awareness about other people. My friend Elisa Joy calls these "Divine Downloads." In this particular case, I was not prepared for the effect my friend's sharing had on my psyche. That evening, I could not sleep. I tossed and turned a large part of the night because I felt very sad for her and her family. When you make the conscious choice to live with an open heart, filled with wonder and curiosity, you feel...very deeply. When I find myself in a place of pain where my heart is very attuned to the discomfort of another, it can hurt...a lot.

The fact that my heart hurt spoke to the love I had for my friend, which is a good thing. In fact, it is a wonderful thing! So, whether it is in the middle of the night or during the day, I shift. I shift my focus; I feel the ache in my body. But, I do not stop there. I know that feeling is a part of living. In order to ease my discomfort, I must be present to what I am feeling. So, I am.

Or, I certainly try to be. I return to my body. I sense where the ache and pain are located. And, I stay with it. I say "yes" to the invitation, as painful as that may be. I breathe. I utter a "thank you" in gratitude. Sometimes, the only answer is to feel... and do nothing.

If we still find ourselves in a place of difficulty, it may mean a look toward our attachments or our ego may be in order. Ego strength is a good, positive thing. It is the place where I end and you begin. However, when your ego is running the show, it can have devastating consequences. How can you tell if your ego is in charge? Well, the ego is often found in a "better than" mindset: anxious, overbearing, wanting its way at all costs. The ego wants others to see and take all the credit for the good in your life. The ego focuses on externals, and without them, it feels lost and empty.

Having appropriate ego strength speaks to understanding it is all grace and love operating the controls of life. Its idea of success is inner fulfillment and connection with others. It does not waver, it is always there for us. It never compares itself with another, because all are created in the image of a loving Creator. It is the place where love expands and does not decrease.

Speaking of love...have you ever been deeply in love? Remember what it was like? You almost forgot yourself because the other was paramount in your mind and heart. That kind of agape love does not destroy your sense of self; it actually increases it. The world looks brighter, crisper, clearer. You feel alive. That is how horses live. They are always fully alive. "The Glory of God is a person fully alive" is a saying attributed to Irenaeus, an early Church Father. This applies to all of the Universe because all of Creation is fully alive. Look at flowers; look at animals; look at your children; look at yourself—magnificent and exquisite!

Recently, I had dinner with a dear friend in Media, Pennsylvania, a quaint town near my home. The center of town holds a "Dining under the Stars" once a week every summer. As we walked by all the diners enjoying their meals outside under the summer sky, I felt so open, so alive. It was as if they were all my friends—friends I had not yet met! Such openness and curiosity create more openness. Sure enough, I did see two friends! This is the secret of the Universe:

When you set your intention with a loving, open, and curious heart, you transform your world into magnificence. How do I know this? Well...you are reading this book right now, aren't you? Something within you chose to say "Yes" to this tome. You are also on your way to magnificence! You are ready to be lifted up!

Chapter 3 Thought Questions

1. How do you create worthiness and value in your life?

2. Can you recall an experience where you realized you were totally loved, chosen, and accepted? Can you remember what it felt like?

3. Do you often have feelings like these (see previous question)? If so, why do you think that is? If not, why not?

4. Do you have areas in your life that may be considered "debris"? If so, which ones? Do you have difficulty moving away from them? If so, why? Can you see the deeper invitation in remaining with the debris? Can you see the invitation in removing the debris from your life?

5. What environment in your life allows you to slow down and fully relax? Do you visit that place/space often? If not, why not?

6. What areas of your life inspire you to love fully? Where is it easiest for you to love? Where is it the most difficult? Can you hold both those tensions with a nonjudgmental and compassionate heart? What does it feel like when you are able to do that? If you are unable to love fully, what tiny step can you take to move toward greater love?

7. Can you recall an experience that made you feel fully alive? How often do you reconnect with that experience? Could you incorporate that image and feeling into your life today?

Chapter 4

Lift

$\mathcal{A}$s you lift your "apple picker," you must lift it away from the ground...you must raise yourself up.

> What does that mean?
>
> How does that apply to your life?
>
> You cannot be raised up until you are able to see where you are right now, in this moment.

Being present to what is, right now, is paramount. Sometimes, we need to get a more distanced perspective by seeing ourselves with a non attached view to gain clarity. Often, we get immersed in drama; we get so attached to our story we cannot see anything else. We focus on it, replaying the script over and over. But every time we compulsively tell and retell a story or drama about ourselves, we are really re-victimizing ourselves.

I think in relation to telling a painful story, balance is the key. For quite a while, years actually, I was immersed in the same story and wanted to make a change but was unable to do so. I would meet with my therapist and hash and rehash what I felt was the same struggle over and over. How patient he was with me!

Eventually, I got tired of listening to myself! The point is, it takes what it takes to move us from a place of being stagnant to making a change. And, no one has the timetable for your life. In my case, the change was accompanied by offering great compassion and kindness toward myself.

This is where lifting is key. You must rise above to get out of the small story and see the larger picture.

We cannot experience clarity when we are narrowly focusing on our own story, which is usually one of discomfort, lack of control, and pain.

We gain clarity when we rise above the discomfort and suffering of the moment.

Dr. Dan Gottlieb, the world-renowned psychologist, says two very profound things (actually, he says lots more, but these linger with me):

"When you are suffering, you need to feel felt."

"You must have a large amount of love in your life to handle the container of suffering."

At its core, *suffering* can be defined as how we feel when things do not go our way. So, right away, we are one with humanity. We are part of a community where everyone you meet is suffering in one form or another. But this is not a reason to live a life of despair. This is a reason to celebrate the amazing world of humanity, which you are an integral part of.

Recently, I experienced the loss of my precious barn dog, Connor. He was a Rottweiler/shar-pei mix, a cross of two rather aggressive breeds. But Connor was the exact opposite. He completely missed the memo that he was supposed to be aggressive. All he knew how to do was love, and that he did, in spades. While living in the barn, the heated and air-conditioned tack room was his home and the couch was his bed. If you sat on that couch, you were *his*. Way too large to be a lap dog, he would nevertheless get as close to you as he could. He would snuggle in so deep you wondered how he could breathe! And his love for all who entered was the gift he offered. He was another four-legged healer at the barn.

When he passed at the young age of six, I was heartbroken. I recall taking him to the vet for the last time. I walked into the office where three women were behind the desk. They scurried to put me into a private room as I was quietly crying at my seat. Two of the three employees were very considerate and compassionate, telling me how sorry they were and that a room was going to be available very soon. The other was working at a computer, and she never even lifted her head in my direction, the direction of suffering. As I quietly sniffled at my seat, before they moved me, I was cognizant of the fact that even though I was crying, she was busily working on the computer and never even looked up.

There could have been many reasons for her not acknowledging me. Perhaps she was very busy. Perhaps she had a computer deadline to meet. Maybe she did not see me. (Hard to believe, but I am trying to stay curious here.) And, perhaps she was not able to be present to someone who was in pain, who was suffering in the moment.

In that place, at that time, as I was sniffling away,

I wanted one thing. I simply wanted her eyes to meet mine. *Can't you see? I am hurting. I need a small semblance of humanity, here. I need to see your eyes. I want to feel felt.* Alas, what I felt I wanted, needed, in that moment did not come. Not from her.

Gratefully, it came from others. It came from the veterinarian who was so present and kind to Connor and me.

As we laid him to rest, he said to me, "Oh, my; this never gets easy."

And I replied, "May it *never* get easy. May it *always* be hard."

This is where humanity is, where we feel felt. When we feel felt, we can continue on and begin to heal. We can see the larger picture beyond our circumstances.

> When you move your eyes from your circumstances, lift, see and notice others, your experience of suffering can transform and be a balm to others. Remember: we are hard-wired for connection. True success comes not just from inner fulfillment but also in connecting with others. Connecting occurs when hearts meet hearts.
>
> Horses offer us the amazing ability to always be present to whatever is being presented to them, and to us. They hold us, they carry us. What a gift that is!

When my students are finished with a lesson, I bring the horses into the barn and tell the students to remain mounted. Then, I have them lean forward until their upper body is resting on the horse's neck. I let them relax there, linger.

And then I say to them, "How many things in life can carry us this way? How many things in life can hold us in this way?"

It is a beautiful thing, to be held and carried.

Let others feel you; be authentic and genuine with your feelings. Make sure you give yourself time and allow yourself to feel, too! We can forget to do that! Feeling your own discomfort is pivotal to living a magnificent life.

Why is that?

Because if you do not allow yourself to be with your own discomfort, you will not be able to be *congruent*. You will present yourself one way when you are actually feeling another way, which can have devastating consequences to your physical and emotional health. If you are continuously incongruent, your body will not know when to believe you! It will always be in a high-stress state. The reverse is also true:

> The more congruent you are, the more you become who you are meant to become; the more capable you are of not over protecting your false self or boundaries. You are able to be free.

Horses are a great model for us in relation to discomfort and incongruence. They are always authentic and genuine. If they are in some discomfort, they will respond in a way to change that and return to a state of satiation. We humans, too can respond accordingly, get the tools to look above our circumstances, and do the next right thing.

I know; that is easier said than done.

Sometimes, *doing the next right thing* means doing nothing. We are a very reactive society! We are always moving to the next task. I think that may be an evasive maneuver, an attempt to deal with our discomfort. We may need to take no action—just feel and be with our feelings. That passive kind of state is actually very active, just in a different way. We need tools to be with our stillness.

My dear friend Tom Herstad told me: "The biggest addiction on the planet is a busy mind." We need to stop, and be still; so we can move into the mindset of being lifted *up*.

To live in a state of being lifted up requires a huge amount of faith and trust, trust that, "All is as it should be," as the *AA Big Book* states.

Julian of Norwich (1342-1416) echoed the same sentiment centuries earlier: "All shall be well and all manner of thing shall be well."

> We have to trust that even in the presence of all that is unknown we have a sense we are being carried and held. We are being lifted up to Something that is higher than us. We can have the courage to say "Yes" to it ALL. Yes to discomfort, to difficulties. Yes to life and love.

Why?

Because it all serves to lift us up for a greater and higher good. Richard Rohr, the Franciscan Father, says: "Life is not about you, you are about life." To stay in that transforming perspective, you must be deeply rooted in the foundation of knowing you are chosen, cherished, and valued. I don't think you can progress to the place of saying "Yes!" to it all without that basic tenet.

The more you say "Yes!" the more you move into the place of your destiny, whom you were created to be. You do not have to protect yourself any more, for you are fully alive, open, and lifted to a higher plane. You have nothing to prove or protect. You *know* you are protected, carried, and held. That is great freedom and great happiness. You can just *be*. That is magnificence!

Before we move on, I want to mention one more pivotal point: intention. *Webster* defines *intention* as "the thing that you plan to do or achieve."

In order to have what you desire come to pass, it must first be birthed within you, as an idea, or thought. Then it must be exposed to the light; you need to say or state your intention. You may not have a clue how it will happen, but you must call it into being.

For years, I have loved Ted Talks. And for years, I told anyone who would listen that I wanted to give one. Consolidating my Resonant Horse workshops into a ten-to eighteen-minute talk would not be easy, I knew. But the message—the incredibly healing message of horses—felt compelled to come out.

I did not know how.

I did not know when.

I just knew I wanted to do it. And so, I would talk about giving a Ted Talk as I went along living my days. Some of my friends probably thought I was nuts. How was I going to make that happen? I had no idea! All I knew I had was my intention.

Flash back to the summer of 2015. I had a session with my therapist who casually mentioned he was going to give a TEDX Talk (TEDX Talks are locally organized Ted Talks). I attended the stellar event, which was held inside a prison. It was such an inspiring day.

I introduced myself to the organizer, a wonderful man with a huge vision. I sent him a follow-up email, thanking him for such a magnificent day. I also mentioned to him the transforming work I do partnering with horses. From there, the ball started rolling. He asked for info, outline, bio, and so on. I sent him the information he requested. Shortly after, I found myself on the roster for a TEDX Talk in Wilmington, DE, in October 2015.

In between the invitation to speak and the actual day was a whirlwind of preparation. After reading the bible of Ted Talks, *Talk Like Ted*, I was practicing and rehearsing to anyone who would listen! I had only two months to prepare, so I had to go the "crash course" route. I

practiced,

practiced,

practiced.

My feelings vacillated from exhilaration to complete, paralyzing fear. One thing I returned to over and over—the way to combat the fear was to be prepared. More practice! I practiced every morning in front of my dog, Harley. He did not seem to mind. I am on staff at a therapeutic center, so I practiced there three times. Nothing more daunting than giving your TEDX Talk before five to twelve therapists!

Eventually, the day came. I had been asked to present first, which was an incredible honor. Unbeknown to the organizer, I had secretly prayed not to have to go last. I could not bear the thought of waiting all day before I presented! What a gift that day was!

Today, I count my TEDX Talk as one of the greatest gifts I could offer. Viewed thousands of times on YouTube, it is my hope that it opens the door for others to view the incredibly healing power of horses.

And it all began with a thought. You must *lift* your thoughts higher, get out of the small story, and feel felt. You must surround yourself with those who allow you to feel felt. You must have intention and a dream.

Before you have a dream, you must dream the dream. Before you have an intention, you must set your intention. Continue to live your life, but be aware that heaven and earth is moving to bring your intention into reality.

Chapter 4 Thought Questions

1. Recall a story or script you play over and over in your life. Let's try a two-minute exercise to enlarge upon the experience and rewire our neurons. Think of an experience where you felt love, connection, safety—anything positive. Stay with it and feel it. Where do you feel it in your body? Go to that place where you feel it the deepest within you. Breathe. Let it grow outward, but still in your body, from where you first felt it. Continue to linger with that positive emotion. Let it embrace your entire body. Notice how good, calm, loving, and safe you feel. Offer a prayer of thanks, as you feel deeply within your body. Continue on with your day, knowing you can revisit this place of positivity anytime.

2. Perhaps your story or script is a negative one. It is difficult to be unattached to a painful story in our lives. With kindness and compassion, visit your negative experience as you did your positive experience in the previous exercise. If emotions are strong, let them ebb and flow. That is the thing with emotions—they are always changing. Repeat this exercise with a strong lens of gentleness. Remember: When we are suffering, we need to feel felt with a loving and nonjudgmental lens. Recall how horses carry and hold us. Ponder that awareness—we are always being carried. Trust there is One who knows us and carries us even in our sorrow—especially in our sorrow.

3. What is your dream that is being birthed within you? What is one step you could take toward bringing your intention into fruition? What is holding you back from taking your dream to the next level?

Chapter 5

Sift

When you were growing up, do you remember watching your parents sift flour? If so, you may have wondered, what is its purpose of this task? Sifting, simply put, lightens the load. It is deeper than picking as it involves a slight shaking, back-and-forth motion. Sifting involves deep discernment.

> Often, when our world gets shaken, it is hard to see the gold that is still there.

At some point, after sifting comes stillness. As a part of humanity, we will have sifting in our lives. Say "Yes" to the invitation, for anything that can be shaken will be shaken. This occurs so that the unshakeable will remain. Sifting involves holding the tension until the load can lighten. It speaks to acceptance, to giving ourselves permission to be in a process, and to acknowledge that right where we are is okay and enough.

I found these principles to be greatly tested in my life when I went through a challenging time getting a divorce. When you are suffering, it is difficult to say "Yes" to the pain, which occurs on so many different levels. Sometimes, I just had to keep putting one foot in front of the other and begin the next right thing. Tending to the horses was a healing balm, for they needed care every day, more than once a day. I *had* to get out of myself, to tend to something other than myself. The horses were silent sentries to my suffering.

That being said, I also found that human support was indispensable to my journey. I immediately involved myself with a support group of those going through a similar life change. While family and friends are important during this time, they cannot really help us with the deep sorrow we are experiencing (in my humble opinion). That is because family and friends are too close to the entire situation. The best help is the support of others *who are going through what you are going through*. I feel that is the pathway to the greatest healing, where you can be with your sorrow and grieve and allow your pain to move you to a deeper place of compassion and empathy.

Support and recovery groups are the unsung heroes of the healing realm. There, those with deep sorrow can be with others to help carry and ease the load. We are comforted when we are able to be with those who need to be comforted. It is amazing how that works!

One of the greatest gifts I received from the support group I attended was an idea of what my ex was going through. That idea allowed me to have compassion for him. He was most likely not aware of that, but I was. I had tools for not reacting and responding. Again, when we are suffering, we need to feel felt. The support of others gave me the space to feel felt.

It was not an easy time, but looking back on it, I see that I was always being carried and supported. Watching the horses, I gained tools for not reacting, for noticing my discomfort, and for being still.

Acceptance is a breeze when life is going our way; not so much when it is not. Here is what we need to know about acceptance: *We cannot change anything until we accept it.*

Acceptance means we say "Yes" even if we are screaming "No" inside. When we are suffering, it is exquisitely difficult to say "Yes." However, if we say "No," we only increase our pain and discomfort.

How does that happen?

It is simple. Since you are human, you experience pain and suffering. Your tendency is to resist it. Now you have two issues to contend with:

1. Your suffering, pain, and so on is most likely due to an event or an occurrence.

2. Your reaction (i.e., lack of acceptance) to said event or occurrence.

When sifting occurs (translation: life happens), just try to accept it. Do not resist. Out of that acceptance can come tools for compassion, mindfulness, and self-care. Whatever you resist will persist. And, when it does, it only adds to your suffering.

So sift, lighten your load
Be still. Accept.
Say "yes."

Angels fly because they take themselves so lightly. Trust, even when it hurts. All will be well. All is well.

Chapter 5 Thought Questions

1. What does support look like to you, right now, in this stage of your life?

   - Emotional support?
   - Spiritual support?
   - Physical support?

2. Are you sufficiently supported in all those areas? In which area(s) is your support the strongest? The weakest? Is there a shift or a change that needs to occur?

3. Can you give an example of when a lack of acceptance increased your pain? How did you respond or react? Could you have seen a greater invitation to growth?

Chapter 6

Remove

Sift and remove have some traits in common, as they both speak to letting go. Sifting determines what stays and what goes, where as removing leads to letting go. We let go of the muck, the manure, the destruction and desolation of our lives. Trust, a thread that runs through the entire mucking process, is now very integral.

> We must trust that when we let go-in the act of letting go, we will be:
> Carried
> Held
> And taken care of.

A while ago, I had stopped and observed four of my horses as they munched on their hay. Three of the horses were eating. One horse was simply standing away from the hay, resting, lingering. As I watched him, I thought, "Oh, my! He has had his fill; he is just relaxing in a satiated state. He is not concerned that there won't be any more hay left for him; he is full, and it is enough."

What is it within him that allows him to be so content, so present to the moment? How was he able to be in a "state of enough"? I want to live in that state! Not just in enough, but in abundance!

At that moment, my horse was not concerned

about getting the last blade of hay. He was OK with the others eating and he was OK with himself not eating. He was living in the world Richard Rohr calls "both/and, not either/or."

Either/or is the narrow worldview some people have. It presents itself when we are young and is needed for healthy growth and boundaries. We are taught to not cross the street without looking both ways. Do not touch a hot stove. These things are very important to know. But, as we age, life has a way of stretching us, causing us to squirm and react to those early constraints. They are important, for sure. But with age comes wisdom, and hopefully, a capacity to allow pain and discomfort and suffering to teach us and soften us. Life becomes a world of *both/and.* You can be suffering *and* be grateful. You can be in pain *and* see where the invitation to growth is.

Horses are *masters* of living in the both/and. Just watch how they deal with the discomfort of, say, flies in the summertime. They swat with their tails; they twitch. Sometimes, if severe enough, they may run away from them, or roll them off. They respond accordingly. They react. And they accept. What a model for us. And, when we can, we help them in their discomfort by offering to apply fly spray to ease their load. What a loving act we offer them.

What a loving act we can offer ourselves by being present to our own discomfort and offering ourselves kindness and compassion.

Recently, I found myself in a place of constant, internal turmoil. On the outside, many wonderful things were happening. But inside, I was a mess of nerves, in-attention, and constantly on the move. For me, when I begin to lose myself, I tend to get busier and move faster. It is as if I am in so much pain that I have to keep busy so I do not feel it.

Of course, the remedy is exactly what I am trying to move away from! The remedy is to slow down, *stop* if need be, and simply feel. And that is what I do. It may take some time, but eventually I always come back to the one I can trust—myself. I can trust myself. The way I slow down is I bring great attention and intention to doing what is the next right thing.

Summertime, as I have mentioned, is a tough time for horses. It comes with lots of bugs and flies out at the barn. Horses need us to treat their bellies so bugs do not congregate there; they need spray and ointment. It is a routine I do often.

We have already spoken about routines. When I am in need of returning to myself, I take a chore like that and I focus on every move I make. As I tend to the horses, I remind myself of what an incredibly loving act it is to care take of them in this way. I do each task with great love and attention.

I move from a place of struggle and resisting to gratitude and grace. As I slow down and focus on every movement,
every lift of my hand,
every step I take.

I return to the moment. I return to what is. I return to the present. It is incredibly grounding and refreshing.

It is the way horses live all the time. What great examples they are for us!

When we are in their presence, we can even become aware of traits we had within ourselves, but did not, at first notice. "Mark" is a bright 18 year old, finding his way in the world of today. We were working in the round pen, and before he went in to be with the horse, I asked him to get in touch with his body and what he was feeling in the moment. Then, I asked him to turn around, and look at the horse. Did he feel differently when he looked at the horse? He said, Yes, bigger." As he entered the round pen and commenced the exercise with the horse, I could see a physical shift within him. He WAS bigger. His energy and his intention was so focused, the horse could do nothing but respond in the loving way he was asking him. And, respond he did, in a beautiful, focused manner. Every time Mark asked for a shift in gait or a transition, the horse altered his pace accordingly. He did it slowly, methodically, responding only to the energy flowing from Mark.

In that moment, the horse was a mirror for what Mark had within him, but the horse aided Mark in bringing it to the surface. Mark always had the ability to be "bigger" but the horse was almost the conduit for bringing it to fruition. It was a lovely time to observe, and my guess is Mark will linger with that experience for a long while. It just may aid him in feeling a bit "bigger" in his world, as well.

Chapter 6 Thought Questions

1. Can you recall a time when you felt utterly and completely cared for and loved? You lacked for nothing in that moment. You were living in a state of enough. Practice living in the world of enough. And, not just enough—but abundance!

2. List five tasks you do every day. The next time you attend to them, give them 100 percent of your attention. What does that feel like? Does it alter the way you view the tasks?

Chapter 7

Remove and Let Go:
Living with an Open Heart,
Healthy Boundaries,
and Kindness

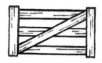

> "The most fortunate are those who have a wonderful capacity to appreciate again and again, freshly and naively, the basic goodness of life with awe, pleasure, wonder and even ecstasy."
>
> Abraham Maslow

To experience those traits daily involves attention to what is right in front of us, in the moment. Horses are such great models for us! We have already discussed how authentic, genuine, and congruent they are. Their evolution through the centuries has brought them to what they are today, to where we can partner with them. We transform our lives by observing their lives.

One particular strength horses have is appropriate boundaries. For example, when they want another horse to move away from a particular hay pile, they move toward the horse with just the right amount of energy and intention. You can see it. The more alpha in the herd uses the least amount of energy because he is, after all, the alpha!

Boundaries are such a hot topic these days and probably an outgrowth of the highly co-dependent decades of the '70s and '80s. I am so grateful when clients come to the farm. We have amazing visual, in-the-moment experiences which offer immediate feedback. In those moments, we see appropriate boundary-setting behavior in action. Having boundaries does not mean you allow people to walk all over you. Nor does it mean your boundaries are so severe you are emotionally shut down. It just defines where the space is between you and another, physically and emotionally. Physically, it is obvious; emotionally, not so obvious.

My friend Bobbie McIntyre, a Licensed Emotional Integration Trainer as well as a Certified Equine-Assisted Life Coach, has this to say:

"I can tell you from personal experience about living with an open heart (without boundaries) and living with boundaries. I fell into the trap (as others do) that living with an open heart is the epitome of love and/or spirituality....I have come to realize that living with an open heart (without boundaries) is *not* empathic and is actually detrimental to self-respect and earning the respect of others."

What tremendous words of wisdom. How lucky we are to have horses aid us in the understanding of what is and is not appropriate. To live with an open heart *and* healthy boundaries is the key!

Mother Teresa has said that "Kindness is the greatest religion." The older I get, the more I agree with her. Kindness can occur in the simplest of ways—a smile, a sigh, a hug. It can be a moment of honoring your own life in all its complexities and challenges.

I hope reading this book has gotten your attention. Of course, I hope the title caught your eye first! Such a frivolous title, but it may have caused you to pick up this book, hopefully chuckle, and actually read it.

You may never set foot inside a stable, let alone muck out a horse stall. Your life may look 100 percent different than mine, and that is totally OK, and wonderful. The principles set forth within these pages are a way to connect to me, to you, and to humanity at large. At our essence, we are much more alike than different. We all breathe. We all ache. We all love. Hopefully, we all connect. And, we are all on a journey.

Wendell Berry says it well:

"A Spiritual Journey"

And the world cannot be discovered
by a journey of miles,

no matter how long,

but only by a spiritual journey,

a journey of one inch,

very arduous and humbling and joyful,

by which we arrive at the ground of
our feet,

and learn to be at home.

(Berry, *The Unforeseen Wilderness,* 43, University Press of Kentucky, 1/1/1971)

My desire for you is for you to find your home. Find the place that you love and that loves you, and then move toward that love, deeply. You have some tools for finding and noticing: Pick, Lift, Sift, Remove, Let Go. I want you to move toward it because that is what the world needs.

The world needs *you.*

It needs to see you loving what you do with every breath you take. It needs to find you, in mundane and simple tasks, honoring yourself and your Creator.

And when you truly find what it is you love and are doing it, please drop me a line! I would love to know how *you* are changing your world!

Chapter 7 Thought Questions

1. List an experience where you have noticed growth within yourself in relation to healthier boundaries. In particular, how did it change the way you viewed yourself?

2. What are your thoughts and opinions of religion? Some have said that religion is "for people who believe in hell...whereas spirituality is for people who have been there." What are your thoughts and feelings about that statement?

3. Do you feel there is a connection between religion, spirituality, and kindness? Do you agree with Mother Teresa's statement: "Kindness is the greatest religion?" If so, why? If not, why not?

4. Recalling Wendell Barry's poem "A Spiritual Journey," how do the last two sentences apply to your life ("...By which we arrive at the ground of our feet, and learn to be at home.")?

About the Author

Mindy Tatz Chernoff grew up in the northwestern suburbs of Chicago, where she rode her pony throughout the forest preserves and through rural neighborhoods. At a very young age, she realized that caring for horses was a valuable and worthwhile endeavor. She began training horses at age 16 and won at countless horse shows, including the prestigious Chicago International Livestock Show.

After graduating from Stephens College, she married and relocated to Philadelphia, PA. As her children grew, she reentered the wonderful world of horses, first teaching, then, as her student base increased, buying and selling quality horses in the Tri-State area. Scores of children in the Philadelphia suburban area grew up under her tutelage, and many of her past students now have children of their own who are riding! In addition, her students are located all over the country and beyond.

While raising her three children and operating two barns, Mindy returned to school, receiving a Dual Masters in 2005. Her degrees in Holistic Spirituality and Spiritual Direction enabled her to offer retreats and individual sessions with a wide, diverse group of clients. She gradually began incorporating principles of mindfulness, dealing with discomfort, and building upon one's positive traits. Instead of teaching clients how to ride, she began to teach them about life while riding.

A serious life change happened, which thrust Mindy into a deeper way of seeing her world, particularly suffering, discomfort and pain. Gradually the horses became a window through her pain, and she is now able to partner with others as they travel their own particular journeys. Mindy's primary goal is to build upon each individual's positive traits, encouraging a sense of calm, contentment and freedom. These are traits which horses, when in a serene environment, live with every day.

Horses evoke a strong sense of authenticity in those who interact with them, and in their environment a client is inclined to slow down, notice, feel and heal. By being in close proximity to horses, under the eyes of a skilled facilitator, stress levels often diminish. People typically experiences deep levels of inner awareness of their feelings and desires.

Mindy's workshops, retreats, one-on-one sessions, as well as her "Horse Circles", all foster a sense of serenity, openness, and curiosity. The offerings at her facility attract entrepreneurs, educators, mental health professionals, business leaders, and her largest demographic — middle aged women in transition. For several years she has been a staff member at Building Bridges, a therapeutic center in Media, PA. Mindy is an Equine Specialist who has years of postgraduate training in mindfulness meditation and executive leadership training. Her continuing education within the Equine Facilitated Leadership field includes an Eponaquest Apprentice, as well as an E3A C2-C3 Practitioner.

In her spare time, Mindy was able to show "Flirtin With Music", her paint/pinto gelding to a Pinto Congress Championship in Tulsa, Oklahoma, not once, but twice, first in 2007, and again in 2010. She also is a jewelry artisan, selling her individual, one of a kind pieces to galleries and private shows.

A sought after speaker, Mindy is the author of several published works. *From Muck To Magnificence* is her first full length book.

She can be reached at:

Theresonanthorse@gmail.com

For more information on her services, visit

theresonanthorse.com

Her TEDX Talk "How Horses Heal, Transform and Empower" can be viewed at:

https://youtu.be/QBZkFquIqog

RESOURCES

This list is purposely understated. The world of Equine Facilitated Learning/Equine Assisted Learning/Equine Therapy is blossoming. One only has to google those terms to see their abundance. I am offering resources that have personally impacted my life in tremendous ways. Many of those mentioned below I count as dear personal friends. All of them represent stellar examples of those who love horses and desire to change the world through that love and knowledge.

Carrie Brady
203-210-7484
Posssibilitiesfarm@gmail.com
www.PossibilitiesFarm.com
Located in Wilton, CT.
Carrie partners with horses to bring out the best in humans through personal and professional development workshops, wisdom circles, equine-assisted reiki, and any other programs the horses help her invent!

E3A: Equine Experiential Education
775-376-2530
e3assoc.org
staff@e3assoc.org
Located in Reno, Nevada.
E3A is an international professional membership organization offering training, certification and resources for the implementation of Equine Assisted Learning (EAL) programs by educators, coaches,

Professional Development trainers and other facilitators. They provide the necessary resources for the promotion and implementation of quality, successful, professional equine experiential education programs.

Brent and Kris Graef
806-282-6950
Brentgraef@yahoo.com
Brentgraef.com
Located in Canyon, Texas
Brent teaches horsemanship through feel. He is passionate about his quest for finding ways to give the horses a better deal; he is equally passionate about treating his students with that same respect.

Shari Jaeger Goodwin
540-364-9505
shari@jaeger2.com
jaeger2.com
Located in Virginia.
Shari is an innovative business strategist, leadership coach and author who partners with her horses for business transformation.

June Gunter
919-333-9961
junegunter@teachinghorse.com
Teachinghorse.com
Located in North Carolina.
June partners with horses to advance the practice of authenticity, collaboration and shared leadership.

Linda Kohanov
520-455-5908
info@eponaquest.com
Eponaquest.com
Located near Tucson, AZ.
Linda teaches internationally and explores the healing potential of working with horses. She offers programs on everything from emotional and social intelligence, leadership, stress reduction and parenting to consensus building and mindfulness. She is also a bestselling author.

Ginny Telego
419-651-6854
info@wagersway.com
wagersway.com.
Located in Ashland, Ohio.
Ginny is the President and Founder of Wager's Way Equine Assisted Action Learning. She is a Certified Advanced Practitioner and Master Trainer with the Equine Experiential Association and travels both in the U.S. and abroad to facilitate learning with horses.

Thorncroft Equestrian Center
Sallie and Saunders Dixon
610-644-1963
info@thorncroft.org
thorncroft.org
Located in Malvern, PA.
Thorncroft's mission is to develop the physical and emotional well-being of all people including those with special needs.

TO CONTACT OR BOOK MINDY TO SPEAK:

Mindy Tatz Chernoff

THE RESONANT HORSE

610-247-0408

TheResonantHorse.com

CPSIA information can be obtained
at www.ICGtesting.com
Printed in the USA
BVOW06*0035210717
489404BV00003B/4/P